HANUKKAH

Eight Nights, Eight Lights

Rabbi lighting Hanukkah candles, 19th c. etching

a JEWISH HOLIDAYS book

hanukkah
eight nights, eight lights

by Malka Drucker
drawings by Brom Hoban

HOLIDAY HOUSE · NEW YORK

Copyright © 1980 by Malka Drucker
All rights reserved
Printed in the United States of America

Library of Congress Cataloging in Publication Data

Drucker, Malka.
    Hanukkah: eight nights, eight lights.

    ([Her Jewish holidays])
    SUMMARY: Introduces the history, customs,
rituals, foods, games, and gifts associated with
the Festival of Lights and includes recipes,
crafts, and puzzles for celebrating the Jewish
holiday.
    1. Hanukkah (Feast of Lights)—Juvenile litera-
ture. [1. Hanukkah (Feast of Lights)]   I. Hoban,
Abrom.   II. Title.   III. Series.
BM695.H3D78   296.4'35   80-15852
ISBN 0-8234-0377-7

FOR SUSAN MEYERS

who always says the right thing at the right time

ACKNOWLEDGMENTS

THE AUTHOR would like to thank the following people for reading the manuscript and giving helpful suggestions: Rabbi Harold M. Schulweis, Rabbi Chaim Seidler-Feller, Adaire Klein, and Vicky Kelman.

She would also like to thank:

Shocken Books, Inc. for permission to reprint "These Singing Lights" from *A Blazing Fountain—A Book for Hanukkah* by David Rosenberg. Copyright © 1978 by David Rosenberg.

The Jewish Publication Society of America for permission to reprint prayers for lighting the Hanukkah candles from *The First Jewish Catalog*. Copyright © 1973.

ABOUT THE PHOTO CREDITS:

Skirball is short for Hebrew Union College Skirball Museum, Los Angeles (Erich Hockley, photographer).

Yivo is short for "from the archives of the Yivo Institute for Jewish Research."

JTS is short for The Jewish Theological Seminary of America.

CONTENTS

TO THE READER

WHEN I was growing up, *Hanukkah* was my favorite holiday. Besides my birthday, it was the most exciting time of year. Each winter I looked forward to hearing the Hanukkah story, lighting the candles, eating *latkes*, playing games, and, of course, getting presents.

My job was to choose, from among the rainbow assortment of delicate twisted candles, which colors to put in the *menorah*. Whether I made a pattern of colors or lined up the candles randomly, they were always beautiful. By the eighth night, the menorah would blaze splendidly, but I would feel a twinge of sadness. Now I would have to wait a whole year to celebrate Hanukkah again.

Writing this book has been a great pleasure because, besides remembering past happy celebrations, I've discovered much about Hanukkah that I didn't know. What I've learned has deepened my joy in the holiday, and I'd like to share these early memories and new ideas with you.

1
HEROES

. . . Not by might nor by power, but by my
Spirit, saith the Lord. . . .

ZECHARIAH 4:6

HANUKKAH, the Feast of Dedication or Festival of Lights that begins on the 25th of *Kislev* (November or December), is a holiday of opposites. On the one hand, the holiday is a delight —eight joyous days of songs, games, candlelight, gifts, and delicious foods. On the other hand, the holiday recalls the violent Hanukkah story about the first great war for religious freedom. This war not only saved the Jewish people from extinction, but it also showed how a small group of brave people triumphed over tremendous odds in their struggle for the right to practice their religious beliefs. The battle was unique, because it was fought not for land but for an idea.

Twenty-four hundred years ago, the Jewish people lived as farmers, shepherds, and grape growers in Judea, the land now called Israel. They believed an invisible god had created the entire world and had given them laws to follow for a good and just life. Three of the most important *mitzvot*, or commandments, were *kashrut, circumcision,* and *Shabbat.*

First, the laws of kashrut meant Jews limited what they ate to remind them life was holy. They didn't kill a calf and its mother on the same day, or eat milk and meat together, out of respect for the relationship between mother and child. To limit the killing of animals for food, they also didn't eat pork, wild animals, or shellfish. Second, they circumcised their male children when they were eight days old to bind them to the Jewish people. This was called a *brit*, which means a covenant or contract. Finally, they rested on Shabbat, the seventh day, to celebrate the creation of the world.

Other peoples at that time worshiped visible gods of nature, whose power and presence could be sensed by everyone. They could feel the warmth of the sun god and praise the rain god for thundershowers. To them, every element of the world represented a god. The idea of just one god who could not be seen puzzled many peoples, including the worldly and sophisticated Greeks, who called the Jews "a nation of philosophers who worship the sky." The Greeks, who valued education, physical beauty, and celebrations, worshiped a family of gods who were supposed to have special powers over the lives and activities of the Greeks.

Alexander the Great, king of Macedonia and Greece and conqueror of much of the known world, admired Greek civilization for its grace and beauty. He introduced the Greek way of life into the countries he invaded, including Egypt and Syria, Judea's neighbors to the north and south. Most people liked the Greek way of life. Soon much of the world was speaking Greek, wearing Greek clothes, and worshiping Greek gods. The conquered peoples became *Hellenized*, which means to be made Greek.

At first the Jews paid no attention to this new force around them. Gradually, though, Hellenization crept in, as some Jews left the agricultural world to take up trade with the Greeks. They returned home with money, new customs, and became the "in crowd" of the Jewish community. Many changed their names to Greek names. Some even underwent painful operations to hide that they were circumcised, in order to compete in nude Greek athletic games.

Other Jews, the traditional *Hasidim*, or *Pietists*, objected to the new life-style. They felt Hellenization was weakening Judaism. Soon Jewish society became divided between the Hellenists and the Hasidim.

After Alexander died in 323 B.C.E., the tiny country of Judea became a battleground between Egypt and Syria because each country wanted to include it in its kingdom. The Egyptian *Ptolemies* in the south ruled it until 198 B.C.E. Then the Syrian *Seleucids* in the north took firm possession of Judea.

Antiochus IV, the Seleucid king who came to power in 175 B.C.E., was less tolerant. He believed the only way he could strengthen his empire against the Egyptians was to have a country in which everyone shared the same beliefs. He insisted that his subjects become Greek. He stamped coins with his face on them and called himself Antiochus Epiphanes— "God Manifest." Everywhere, he erected altars to *Zeus*, king of the sky and chief of the Greek gods, to encourage conversions. He built a gymnasium in Jerusalem near the great Temple, where the Jews held their celebrations. The Hasidim were horrified, but the Jewish Hellenist priests ar-

Colossal Seated Zeus

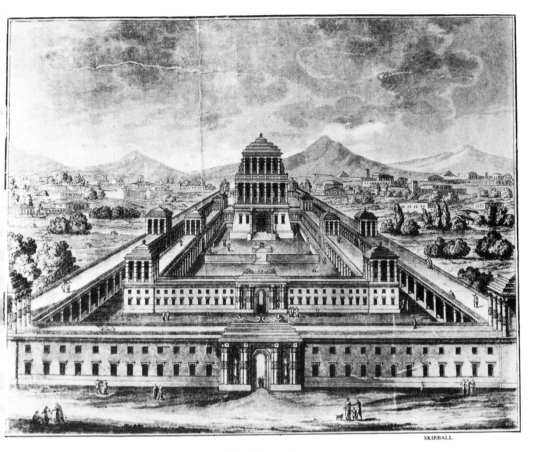

The Temple

gued that there was no harm in physical exercise. Many left
their work in the Temple to wrestle naked in the gymnasium.
The Hellenists believed that Jewish law was a barrier between the Jews and the rest of the empire.

Antiochus decided the best way to control the Jewish community was to appoint his own High Priest. The High Priest
was descended from Aaron and advised the Jewish people in
every aspect of life, from the correct price to charge for wheat
to the proper way to pray. Antiochus chose Jason, who was a
descendant of a priestly family, but who also had embraced
Greek ways and had changed his name from the Hebrew
Joshua. Antiochus promised him he would be rewarded for
his success in Hellenizing the Jews.

Jason believed that Hellenization was to the Jews' advan-
tage, and his first official act was to change the name of
Jerusalem to Antiochea. Many followed his suggestion to
worship both the god of the Jews and the Greek god Zeus.
Jason and his followers argued that Antiochus didn't want to
erase the Jewish people, only the Jewish laws. The Hasidim
believed it was the same thing.

Jason ruled for three years, but Antiochus was not satisfied
with his performance. Hellenization was not happening
quickly enough to please the king. So Antiochus replaced
Jason with his own leader, Menelaus, who robbed the Temple
to pay for his office. He was a corrupt man who pressed hard
to destroy Judaism and spread Hellenism. His appointment
sparked a civil war between the followers of Jason and the
followers of Menelaus. Menelaus won, and a reign of terror
began in Jerusalem. When a rumor spread that Antiochus had
been killed in Egypt, Jason organized an uprising and Menelaus fled. But Antiochus was not dead. Enraged by Jason's

attack on Jerusalem, he punished the uprisers by killing 40,000 Jews. Then he banned all Jewish observance, including kashrut, circumcision, and Shabbat. Holy books were burned, mothers and circumcised babies were murdered, and Jews were forced to eat swine or die. Antiochus became the first leader in history to engage in religious persecution.

The holy Temple was robbed of its riches and the altar was destroyed and replaced with statues of Zeus and offerings of pigs. The Jews went into mourning.

Stories of heroism spread among the Jews and gave them courage. One *midrash* (legend) tells of Hannah and her seven sons. They had been forced to face Antiochus on his throne in the Temple. Abraham, at fifteen, was the oldest and first to come before the king. He refused to bow before the altar, and quoted the Bible: "Thou shalt have no other gods before me." The soldiers tortured and killed him in front of his mother and brothers. One by one, the rest of Hannah's sons were brought before Antiochus and told to bow before the idol of Zeus. Each refused, and each was killed.

David, the second youngest, had seen his brothers murdered and was frightened. Wavering, he turned to his mother and saw her watching him, expecting him to be as brave as his brothers. He turned back to Antiochus and said, "No, I won't bow to these images. There is only one God. Hear, O Israel, the Lord our God, the Lord is One." He too was killed, and Hannah sobbed.

The last child, Solomon, was so beautiful that the king whispered in his ear, "Be as wise as Solomon after whom you were named, and listen to me. I will adopt you as my son and you shall have whatever you desire. You will be a prince."

"No," said Solomon, not yet three years old.

"All you have to do is bend to pick up my ring," the king pleaded. Hannah interrupted to chide the king for trying to trick such a little child. She reminded him that it was he whose hands were wet with blood, not hers. Stung by her words, Antiochus shouted to Solomon, "If your mother will not spare you, then neither will I! Take him away!"

Hannah asked permission to hold the boy one last time. When she hugged him, her heart weakened and she begged the king to kill her first. "It is written in your *Torah* that a mother and her child should not be killed on the same day," Antiochus taunted.

"Have you obeyed all the commandments in our Torah that you also wish to obey this one?" Hannah asked. The last child was taken from his mother. Hannah left the Temple, and in her grief jumped to her death from the Temple wall.

Whether this story actually happened is not important. What matters is that it shows how loyalty and commitment were as important to the survival of the Jews as their beliefs. Even though there were Jews who found it easier to give in, many were determined to overthrow the cruel Syrian ruler at any cost.

In 167 B.C.E., Syrian soldiers came to the village of Modin about thirteen miles north of Jerusalem, to meet with the elderly and respected priest of the *Hasmonean* family, Mattathias. With flattery and promises of position and wealth, the soldiers tried to coax the old man, standing with his five sons, to come to an altar where they had erected a statue of Zeus. They wanted him to kill a pig and eat some of it, thereby setting an example for the others in the village. But Mattathias would not obey. He answered: "Though all the nations that are under the king's dominion obey him and fall away every

"Judah Maccabee," ca. 1960 by Mitchell Siporin

one from the religion of their fathers, and give consent to his commandments, yet will I and my sons and my brethren walk in the covenant of our fathers. God forbid that we should forsake the law and the ordinances. We will not hearken to the king's words to go from our religion, either on the right hand or the left."

Suddenly a villager, tempted by the soldiers' promises of

riches, stepped in front of the altar to offer a sacrifice to Zeus. Enraged at this traitor, Mattathias struck and killed him and then killed a soldier. Tearing down the altar, he thundered, "Whoever is for the Lord, follow me!" Then he and his sons, along with a few followers, fled to the mountains and planned their attack on Antiochus. This is how the *Maccabean* rebellion began.

Mattathias did not kill because he hated Hellenism. He hated being forced to worship gods in whom he did not believe. As a pious Jew, he felt he had the right and obligation to obey God's laws. He did not understand why he could not be a loyal citizen to Antiochus and still follow Jewish laws.

From the hills of Judea, Mattathias and his sons—called the Maccabees, which means "hammers"—led a small group of guerrillas to fight the thousands of Syrian soldiers from Antiochus' powerful army. When Antiochus heard of the growing strength of this group, he sent his soldiers to overpower them. They chose Shabbat for their attack.

The Jews would not fight on their day of rest, and over a thousand of them were killed. Mattathias was grieved and torn by indecision. He knew that this must never happen again, yet he didn't want to violate the Sabbath. At last he told his soldiers that they were not to attack on the Sabbath, but that they could defend themselves.

Soon after this Mattathias, who was then over a hundred years old, died and Judah Maccabee, his son, took his place. He and his small band won victory after victory over the mighty Syrians. They fought with sticks and stones and farm tools sharpened into weapons. The Syrians fought with swords, javelins, and spears and used elephants as tanks. Their soldiers were experienced and ruthless.

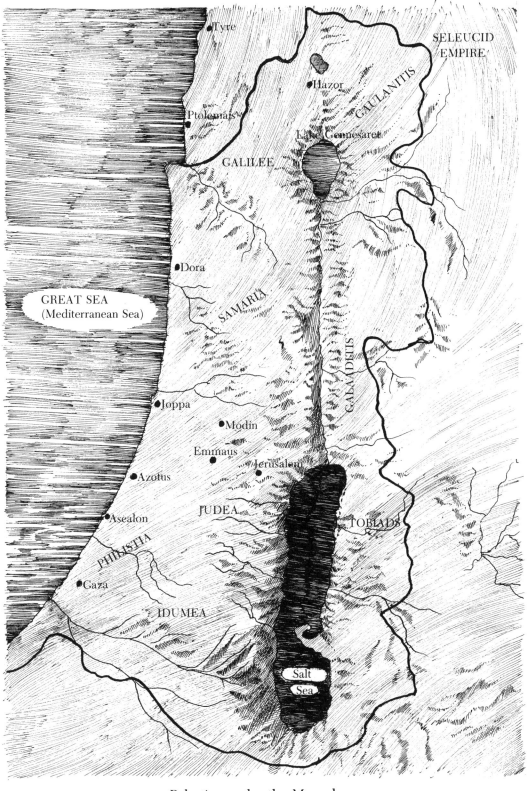

Palestine under the Maccabees

Why were the Maccabees successful? First of all, they knew the country so well they could hide easily from the Syrians and stage surprise attacks. They also knew if they did not win, the Jews would be erased from the earth. But most of all they believed Judah Maccabee's words: "Victory in battle does not depend on the size of an army, but on strength from Heaven."

As the Maccabees grew stronger, Antiochus grew desperate. He never expected the small guerrilla uprising to threaten his plans. He chose Lysias, his most trusted assistant, to lead half his army to wipe out the Maccabees.

Lysias appointed the Syrian generals, Gorgias and Nicanor, to take 20,000 soldiers and elephants to defeat the Maccabees on the Judean plain near the town of Emmaus. When they failed, Lysias took command of the battle himself. The fight was now in the hills, and Judah and his army of 10,000 were able to beat the Syrians by staging sneak attacks from the hills. Frightened by the fervor and power of the Maccabees, Lysias retreated back to Syria, and the Maccabees triumphantly marched into Jerusalem.

It was the 25th of Kislev, 165 B.C.E., exactly three years to the day that Antiochus had first plundered the Temple. Blood, dirt, and ashes had replaced the holy books, altar, and seven-branched Temple menorah. The Temple had to be restored before the Jews could celebrate. They rebuilt the altar, planted new trees in the courtyard, hung new curtains for the holy ark, and relit the menorah, which was supposed to burn constantly. When they were finished, they celebrated for eight days with prayers of thanksgiving, psalms, and fruit offerings. This was the first Hanukkah, which means "dedication." The rededication of the Temple was a rededication of Jewish life. The Maccabees decreed that the eight days following the 25th

The Maccabees rebuilding the Temple, Theodor Galle engraving

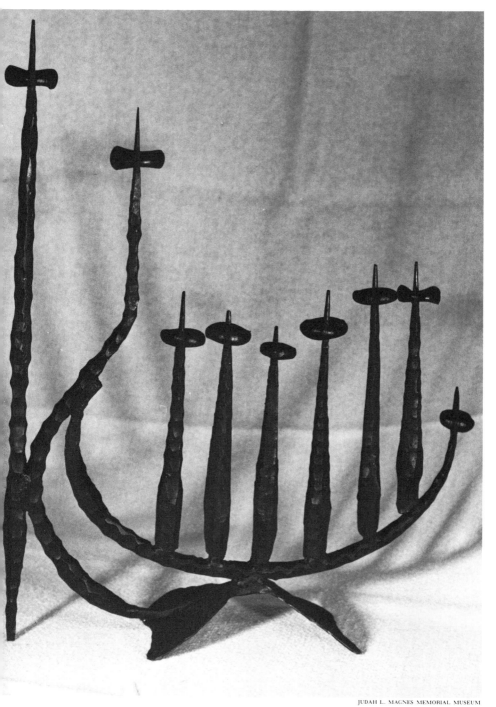

Modern spear-like menorah by David Polumbo

day of Kislev be kept forever as a joyous festival in memory of this event.

Everything in the story so far is factual. But Hanukkah still has its mysteries. No one knows why the Maccabees celebrated for eight days. Some rabbis think the Maccabees were celebrating a belated *Sukkot*, the eight-day harvest festival in the month of *Tishri* (October); they had been too busy fighting to celebrate Sukkot on time. One midrash explains that when Judah Maccabee searched for the sacred oil to relight the Temple menorah, he could find only enough oil to last for one day. The oil miraculously lasted for eight days.

Another midrash, less miraculous but closer to the meaning of Hanukkah, describes how the Maccabees found eight spears on the floor of the Temple. They set them upright, poured oil over them, and turned them into torches. Tools of war became holy Temple lights.

What these stories try to say is that the celebration was not for the military victory, but for the miracle of the inner spirit that gave the Maccabees courage and strength against nearly hopeless odds. This is not a magical or supernatural miracle, but something inside everyone, the spirit to choose what is hard or dangerous but what a person believes to be right.

The battle for religious freedom had not been won forever on the 25th day of Kislev. It was a fight that would be fought over and over, but the Maccabean victory gave the Jews hope. If the Maccabees, a small light in darkness, could win, future generations of Jews also could survive. And though they have had to fight many battles because of their beliefs, the Jewish people still live.

2
Lights

Let there be light.

GENESIS 1:3

As a seed is buried in the earth before it grows, and a baby is in the womb nine months before it's born, darkness comes before light. Because the world began and life begins in darkness, Jewish holidays begin at sundown with the lighting of candles. For Hanukkah, this has special meaning, because the Maccabees brought the light of courage to a world dark with evil and injustice.

Hanukkah candles stand for spirit, courage, justice, and hope. A candle gives off a tiny light, but it has the power to light another candle. And when it does, its own light increases at the moment of contact. Mattathias was the first candle to spark the fight against religious tyranny.

Every year Jews all over the world link themselves to the long chain of their tradition by lighting the *hanukkiyyah*, the

Rabbi at Hanukkah service

Hanukkah menorah. It has eight places for a separate flame—the flames must not touch—and a ninth place for an extra flame called the *shammash*, or "servant" candle, which lights the others. The shammash can be located anywhere, but is usually set apart from the other candles by being higher or farther away.

The light of the Hanukkah candles is not to be used for

work or play. The burning candles are only to be a reminder of Judah Maccabee's fight for religious freedom. That is why there is a shammash, because the other candles may not be used to light one another.

The Hanukkah menorah was first hung in the doorway of the house, "to proclaim the miracle," but today most people put the menorah in a window facing the street. This also lets passers-by know what night of Hanukkah it is. The candles are lit at nightfall, when it's late enough for them to bring light to a darkened room but early enough for everyone in the family, including the babies, to see the ceremony. It's good if each family member has a separate hanukkiyyah, but even if there is only one, each person should have a chance to light the candles. The rabbis said the miracle was for all of us.

On the first night, an unlit candle is put at the far right end of the menorah, perhaps because Hebrew is read from right to left. Each night another unlit candle is added to the left of the preceding candle. That way each candle has its own night. After the shammash is lit, it is used to ignite the candles one by one every night, starting with the candle farthest to the left and moving toward the right.

Forty-four candles burn during Hanukkah, and these small, pretty candles are a reminder that even the small, if they stand together, can light the darkness.

When the holiday was just beginning, the rabbis were unsure whether the number of candles ought to increase each night or decrease. Should they begin with eight candles and burn one less each night? Or should they begin with one, as is done now, and increase each night? Hillel, the great Jewish teacher, settled the question, saying, "In things that are holy we go higher, not lower."

YIVO

3rd-century clay menorah

Because there are Jewish prayers for nearly everything—for different foods, for the first flower of the season, for new clothes, even for earthquakes—it is natural that there is a blessing for one of God's holiest gifts, light. As soon as the shammash is lit, two blessings are said. Everyone has his or her head covered during the blessings to show respect for God.

The first is a blessing over the Hanukkah candles:

Blessed are You, Lord our God, King of the Universe, Who has sanctified us with His commandments and commanded us to kindle the light of Hanukkah.

19th-century oil-burning menorah

The second blessing gives thanks for the miracles:

Blessed are You, Lord our God, King of the Universe, Who performed miracles for our ancestors in those days, at this time.

On the first night, a third prayer is added to give thanks for being able to celebrate the holiday. This prayer is also said at the beginning of most holidays and at new and happy events:

We thank You too, dear God, for keeping us alive and in good health so that we are able to celebrate this festive day.

On Friday night, the beginning of Shabbat, the Hanukkah candles are lit before the Shabbat candles, because flame—a symbol of creativity and work—should not be kindled once the day of rest begins. On Saturday night, the Hanukkah candles are lit after *Havdalah*, the ceremony ending the Sabbath, is finished.

The candles, which must burn for at least a half-hour, spark the imagination. In a darkened room they suggest they are more than candles. Each seems to have its own life, burning brighter or faster than the ones beside it. Sometimes they look like soldiers in different colors, standing straight in a row, with flaming, shimmering helmets.

After the blessings, many families sing songs. Here are two of them.

THESE SINGING LIGHTS (*Ha-Nerot Halalu*)

These singing lights
we light to remember
the miracle of our survival
the miraculous victories and deliverances
out of wars and ashes
that sang in the eyes of our mothers and fathers
at these very days of the year
just as the priests used to sing in the Temple
in ancient days.

Through the full eight days of Hanukkah
these singing lights are deeply felt
for their light is not to see by
not to use in the ordinary world
but to behold and feel

Children singing around Hanukkah candles

like a memory deep within—
like a chord of praise
struck by light
inspiring us to sing
in the name of what's held holy
that we have been delivered to this day
in the miracle of our lives.

Bokharans singing "Rock of Ages"

ROCK OF AGES (*Ma'oz Zur*)

Rock of Ages, let our song
Praise Thy saving power;
Thou amidst the raging foes,
Wast our sheltering tower.

Furious they assailed us,
But Thine arm availed us,
And Thy word
Broke their sword
When our own strength failed us.

Besides the home ceremony, there are prayers of praise, psalms of thanksgiving, and special passages from *Zechariah* that are read in the synagogue during the regular daily services. A large Hanukkah menorah, as well as the seven-branched menorah, is also lit at this time.

The reason why lights became part of the Hanukkah celebration is a mystery, but the clues point to the calendar. Thousands of years before the first Hanukkah, pagan peoples celebrated the winter solstice with bonfires. The fires were lit to rekindle the cold winter sun and to light up the long winter nights. The Greeks also held great revels of *Dionysus*, the Greek god of wine, at that time of year. They celebrated with torches of fire.

The Jews knew of these celebrations and borrowed from them, but fire took on a different meaning at Hanukkah. More than simply a way of warming the sun, fire became a symbol of holiness and rededication. There are still nature roots to the Hanukkah celebration, though. Just as the hanukkiyyah grows brighter each day of Hanukkah, so the sun increases its light each day of winter until the days are long again. During the winter Hanukkah is a small light that warms and cheers us.

"Kindling of Hanukkah Lamp in a Polish-German Home"
by K. Selsenhardt, Poland, 1893

3
GAMES

A great miracle happened there.

MESSAGE OF THE DREIDEL

THE rabbis set the laws for Hanukkah, but the people made the holiday sweet and fun. They couldn't work by the Hanukkah lights, so they found the time perfect for playing games. Although the rabbis didn't encourage playing at any time, they relaxed the rules at Hanukkah.

Dreidel, the most popular Hanukkah game, began when Antiochus forbade the Jews to study Torah, the Jewish Bible. Groups of boys who had memorized the entire Torah would secretly study together until they heard the footsteps of the Syrian soldiers. Then they would quickly pull out spinning tops called dreidels and pretend to be playing games.

In the Middle Ages, dreidel playing became more complicated as rules were borrowed from a German gambling game played with a four-sided top with a different letter on each

18th-century wooden Polish dreidel

19th-century wooden
German dreidel

side. The Jewish version used the letters, **בּ** (*nun*), **גּ** (*gimmel*), **הּ** (*he*), and **שּ** (*shin*), which stood for *Nes gadol hayah sham* ("A great miracle happened there"). Although the rabbis especially disapproved of gambling, they accepted the dreidel because of this Hanukkah message. They also discovered another religious connection. Each Hebrew letter has a numerical equivalent and the four letters on the dreidel add up to 358, the same number as the letters of the word "messiah." The rabbis interpreted this to mean that the messiah would show the way for future miracles.

In the days before dreidels were manufactured, children spent weeks carving their own dreidels from wood they found in nearby forests. Now dreidels can be bought in many sizes and materials, including redwood, silver, and plastic. Generally, the smaller dreidels spin better than the larger ones. Any number of people can play, and each player is given an equal number of objects—pennies, nuts, or raisins.

To start the game, everyone takes five objects from his or her pile and puts them into the main pile. Then everyone takes turns spinning the dreidel. This is what each spin means:

NUN: Do nothing.
GIMMEL: Take the main pile.
HE: Take half the main pile.
SHIN: Give half of your pile.

Players who have nothing left to give are out of the game, and the player who outlasts the others is the winner. The game can be made harder by drawing a circle, two feet in diameter. The players must try to keep the spinning dreidel inside the circle. If it falls outside, the player loses a turn.

WIDE WORLD PHOTOS

Dreidel spin

Dreidel can also be played just as a spinning game. Whoever spins the dreidel the longest is the winner. Another dreidel game uses the numerical equivalents of the four letters on the dreidel: *nun*, 50; *gimmel*, 3; *he*, 5; and *shin*, 300. Each player takes turns spinning the dreidel and the first player to reach 1,000 wins.

The spin of the dreidel is important in another way, too. The world is like a spinning dreidel: Everything happens in cycles. As the earth spins on its axis, the seasons change, and so do the fortunes of people. Antiochus the mighty fell when the small army of Maccabees overturned his rule.

Besides dreidel games, ordinary games such as cards and dominoes are played, too. And familiar board games are often turned into Hanukkah games. The opposing pieces in chess and checkers become the Maccabees battling the Syrians. Scrabble becomes Hanukkah Scrabble by giving 25 bonus points for words related to Hanukkah, such as "candle," "light," and "miracle." Number riddles called *kattoves* were also traditional Hanukkah amusements. A question based on the Torah was asked, and the answer always equaled 44.

When the Maccabees won liberty in Judea, they threw away the coins with Antiochus' image on them and stamped Judah Maccabee's portrait on their own family coins. This is why Hanukkah *gelt* (money) is part of the holiday. Some families have a treasure hunt of coins hidden around the house. Everyone keeps the treasure he or she uncovers. Even hide-and-seek has special meaning at Hanukkah, because it is a reminder of how the Maccabees hid from the Syrians in the hills and caves of Judea.

4
FOODS

When you eat and take pleasure in the taste and sweetness of food, bear in mind that it is the Lord who has placed into the food its taste and sweetness. You will then truly serve Him by eating.

BAAL SHEM TOV

SOMETIMES when you remember a special happy time, you can almost smell your memory. A whiff of popcorn might remind you of the circus, or a roasting turkey might remind you of Thanksgiving at your grandparents' house. Hanukkah smells like latkes, small potato pancakes that are fried in oil. Although the tradition of eating them at Hanukkah began in Eastern Europe, some say they are a reminder of the Maccabean women who cooked latkes for the Jewish soldiers.

Because they are fried in oil, latkes are eaten at Hanukkah to remember the tiny jug of oil that miraculously lasted for eight

45

days. They can be eaten at any time, but somehow they taste best at Hanukkah.

Before you begin cooking, it's a good idea to have an adult around. Frying with oil is a tricky business.

LATKES

3 large potatoes
1 small onion
2 beaten eggs
2 tablespoons flour
1 teaspoon salt
pinch of pepper
½ cup vegetable oil

Wash the potatoes very well, but don't peel them. Grate them coarsely into a bowl. Grate in an onion. Add the beaten eggs, flour, salt, and pepper. Let the mixture sit for ten minutes to thicken. Pour off excess liquid. Heat the vegetable oil for one minute in a frying pan, then drop teaspoonfuls of the mixture into the pan. When the pancakes are brown around the edges, turn and fry them until the other sides are crispy. Drain them on paper towels and eat them with sour cream and applesauce.

APPLESAUCE

6 apples
sugar

Wash the apples, cut them into quarters, and remove the cores. Place the pieces in a saucepan and partly cover them

with water. Simmer the apples until they are soft. Put them in a blender, skin and all. Blend them until the mixture looks like applesauce. (If you don't have a blender, remove the skin and mash the boiled apples with a fork.) Don't overblend, or you'll end up with baby food. Put the blended apples back into the saucepan and add enough sugar to make them taste sweet. Cook them gently for three minutes. A little cinnamon gives them a tangy taste.

In Israel, the traditional Hanukkah treat is not latkes, but *sufganiyyot*, orange-flavored doughnuts fried in oil.

SUFGANIYYOT

¾ cup orange juice
¼ pound margarine (115g)
¼ cup sugar (50g)
2 packages dry yeast
3 cups flour (420g)
2 beaten eggs
dash of salt
vegetable oil
powdered sugar

Mix together the orange juice, margarine, and sugar. Heat the mixture until the margarine melts. Cool it to lukewarm and sprinkle in the yeast. Stir the mixture until the yeast dissolves. Add the flour, eggs, and salt and mix them until you get a smooth dough. Knead (punch and fold over) until the dough is springy. If the mixture is too sticky, add more flour. Place the dough in a greased bowl and let it rise for a half-hour. Punch it down and shape it into small balls or doughnut rings. Let them rise for another half hour. Fry them in two inches of hot oil until they're golden brown. Drain them on a paper towel. Put some powdered sugar in a paper bag, add the doughnuts, and shake.

Hanukkah is a perfect time for parties. It gives families and friends a chance to get together. Any one of the eight nights is fine for exchanging gifts, singing songs, and enjoying special holiday foods with others. Besides latkes and sufganiyyot, "Maccabee sandwiches" are fun to serve because they look as good as they taste.

Begin with a round slice of tomato for Judah Maccabee's head. Use fresh peas for his eyes and mouth. A short piece of celery makes a good neck and a whole wheat sandwich makes a nice middle. If you're serving it at the same time as the sour

cream with latkes, the sandwich should have a dairy filling, because meat and milk are not served together, according to the laws of kashrut. This leaves many choices, including peanut butter and jelly, egg salad, or jack cheese with avocado. Cut small radishes for buttons on the jacket. Try using fat carrot pieces for the arms and legs, and an asparagus spear for an impressive sword.

Butter cookies are also delicious for Hanukkah parties because the butter is a kind of fat that burns, and is another reminder of the oil that burned for eight days.

BUTTER COOKIES

6 to 8 tablespoons butter
1/3 cup of sugar (75g)
1 egg
1 cup white flour (140g)
1/3 teaspoon salt
½ teaspoon vanilla extract

Blend the butter and sugar until they are creamy. Beat in the egg, flour, salt, and vanilla. Chill the dough for several hours. Preheat oven to 375° F. (190° C.). Roll the dough on a board and cut out the cookies with a drinking glass. Or shape the dough into one-inch balls and flatten them with the bottom of a glass. Place them on a greased cookie sheet and bake them for ten to twelve minutes.

Cheese is also traditional at Hanukkah, although the reason is not appetizing. Judith, a cousin of the Maccabees, was a

very beautiful woman. Women were feeding and hiding the soldiers, but they weren't actively fighting the Syrians. Judith wanted to do more to help. She knew that the Syrian general Holofernes liked her very much and would be flattered by her attention.

One night, she took a large basket of food and went to visit the general in the hills above her village. When she got to his camp, the guards stopped her, but Holofernes greeted her with open arms. She smiled sweetly at him, and he was

"Judith and Holofernes" by Andrea Mantegna

encouraged by her warmth. He invited her to eat with him, but she explained she could eat only food prepared according to the laws of kashrut, so she had brought enough for both of them. Holofernes accepted her gracious gift and invited her into his tent, where they dined alone.

Judith had packed a dairy meal, heavy with cheese and salt. Holofernes ate a great amount of the food and drank a lot of wine to quench his thirst. Judith smiled sweetly at him while he ate, and Holofernes was delighted. After a while, though, the wine made him sleepy. He became very tired and, though he tried to keep his eyes from closing, he soon fell asleep.

Judith didn't waste time. As soon as she saw that he had fallen into a drunken sleep, she prompty unsheathed his knife and cut off his head. Judith then ran from the tent and escaped back to her village, where she triumphantly displayed Holofernes' head to her relatives.

You may not want to think of this story while you eat cheese at Hanukkah.

19th-century Polish silver oak tree menorah

5
CRAFTS

"This is my God and I will glorify Him."

EXODUS 15:2

WHEN Hanukkah menorahs were made by hand, there were as many types of hanukkiyyot as there were makers. Images of elephants, bears, lions (symbols of Israel), and Judith beheading Holofernes have been found on different menorahs. Sometimes a menorah was as humble as a potato cut lengthwise, with five holes in one half and four in the other.

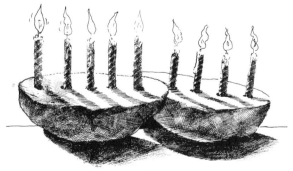

If people had a choice, though, most would make or buy the nicest hanukkiyyah they could. For many artists, the menorah inspired extraordinary designs. The earliest menorahs were made in Middle Eastern countries 200 years after the first Maccabee Hanukkah. They were small, pear-shaped oil lamps made of clay. One lamp was added each night in the doorway. Later the lamps were attached to make a single candelabrum that hung on the left doorpost.

The most popular design for the candle-burning hanuk-kiyyah was taken from the standing Temple menorah, which resembled a tree with seven branches, one for each day of the week. The menorah was supposed to be like a tree of life, whose fruit stands for light and knowledge. It combined earthly strength with heavenly light.

Most menorahs today are machine-made, but the tradition encourages making your own menorah. It can hang or stand, use oil or candles, and be made of a material that won't burn, like metal or clay. The candle or oil holders should be far enough apart so the flames won't touch one another. Usually, the shammash stands apart from the others by being set higher, lower, or farther away. The flame holders don't even have to be connected. You can make eight separate lions and one elephant of clay or modeling dough, and change their position each night. One night the eight lions can be in a circle with the elephant shammash in the center, and another night they can be in a straight line with the elephant in front. While the clay is soft, press a candle into each figure to make the hole.

An unusual Hanukkah menorah can be made from a distributor cap for an eight-cylinder car. Hanukkah candles fit perfectly into the nine holes. Maybe you can get an old one from a gas station.

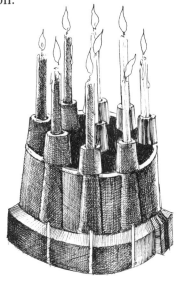

Another way to make a menorah from everyday objects is to use bottle caps. You need a piece of wood 1 foot (30.48 centimeters) long and 2½ inches (6.35 centimeters) wide, and nine aluminum bottle caps. Place the bottle caps on the wood, top down, in an interesting design. Then glue them in place with plenty of white glue. Fill the caps with olive oil and 5-inch (12.7-centimeter) wicks, or fit candles into them.

A hanukkiyyah made of natural objects does two things. First, it fulfills the mitzvah of lighting the candles, and second, it unites two important parts of Hanukkah, the story of the Maccabees, and the winter fire festivals from which the Maccabees borrowed customs for the first Hanukkah. A very simple natural menorah can be made from nine halves of walnut shells containing olive oil and wicks. Iraqi Jews use a walnut menorah, but they use melted butter instead of olive oil.

The materials for an acorn menorah can be found on a trip to the woods. Look for a thick piece of bark—pine is especially good—approximately a foot (30.48 centimeters) long. A fallen tree branch that lies flat will also work. Then gather

the bottoms of nine fat acorns and soak them for two hours in a solution of alum (from a hardware or drugstore) and water. This flameproofs the acorns. When the acorns are dry, glue them to the flat side of the bark with white glue. If there's room on the bark, glue down bits of moss and lichen for decoration. This menorah burns only candles, because acorns are too small to hold enough oil to burn for a half-hour.

These menorahs are simple and can be made anywhere, by anyone, which is what the rabbis intended. They wanted everyone, no matter how poor, to light the Hanukkah candles.

Besides the menorahs, you can make decorations for the house. But first a suggestion: Don't overdo it! Hanukkah is not a major celebration for Jews as Christmas is for Christians. A few decorations here and there rather than a whole lot are appropriate to the spirit of this happy but minor holiday.

The easiest decorations to make are chains made from rings of paper that link together. Make the rings by joining the ends of strips of construction paper with glue, staples, or tape. If you make the chains long enough, you can string them across the ceiling. You can make them from blue or white paper or

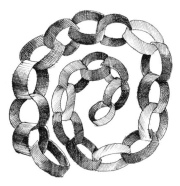

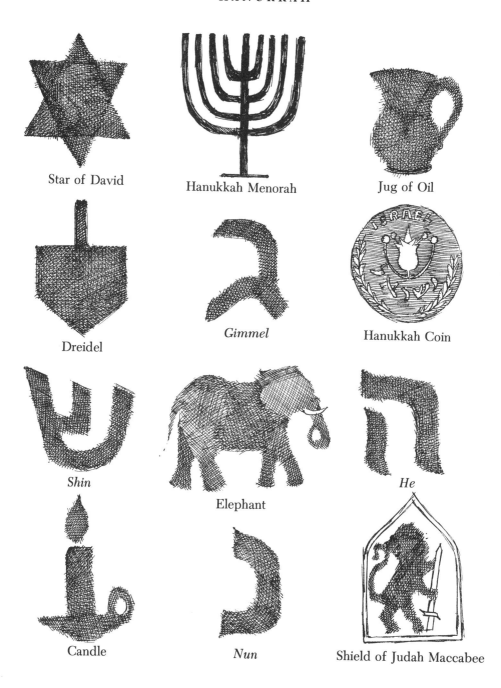

Star of David

Hanukkah Menorah

Jug of Oil

Dreidel

Gimmel

Hanukkah Coin

Shin

Elephant

He

Candle

Nun

Shield of Judah Maccabee

from multicolored strips cut from magazines. Blue and white are traditional decorative colors in Judaism, because blue is considered a royal color and white a humble one. The Torah says that the Jews are to wear blue-and-white fringes, since they are a nation of priests who are humble servants of God.

On the facing page there are a dozen different Hanukkah designs. These designs can be enlarged and cut out for wall decorations, and are also appropriate for use in making print blocks. With a pen, copy a design onto a gum eraser. Then cut away the background with a hobby knife. It's a good idea to have an adult help with this part. You can also carve more details into the design itself. When the block is finished, press it onto an ink pad (they come in different colors in stationery stores) and then onto a piece of paper. The design should stand out clearly. You can make Hanukkah wrapping paper

by stamping white butcher paper. You can also use the stamp to make Hanukkah cards: Fold a sheet of white typing paper into fourths and stamp the cover. Write "Happy Hanukkah" or your own message inside.

If you make nine block designs, you can create a Hanukkah Bingo game. First cut eight square pieces of cardboard or posterboard. Then, with a ruler and marker, divide each square card into nine boxes. Stamp a Hanukkah design in each box, making sure not to repeat a design on any single card. Also, do not stamp the designs in the same order on the different cards, so that when you are done no two cards will look exactly the same. Now cut a piece of paper into nine squares and stamp a different design on each. One person, known as the caller, should put the paper squares in a bag and shake them up. Everyone else takes a stamped playing card. Then the caller pulls out one paper square at a time from the bag and announces the name of the design to the players. The players then look for that design on their cards and cover it

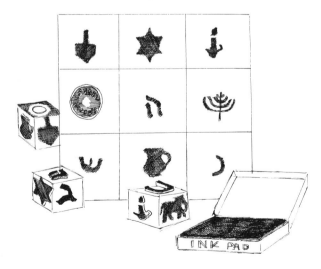

with a penny. The first person to have three designs covered in a straight or diagonal row shouts "Hanukkah!" and is the winner.

Although it's hard to make a fast dreidel without carpentry tools, here is an idea for a spinning dreidel that can also be used as a fancy container for chocolates, Hanukkah gelt, or a small gift. On a piece of construction paper, draw this pattern:

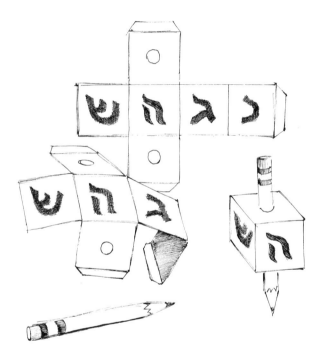

Cut on the outlines, and then fold on the inside lines. Tape the flaps to form a box. Put in candy or a coin before the last flap is taped. If you put a small hole in the top and bottom of the dreidel, and stick a sharpened pencil through it, the dreidel will spin.

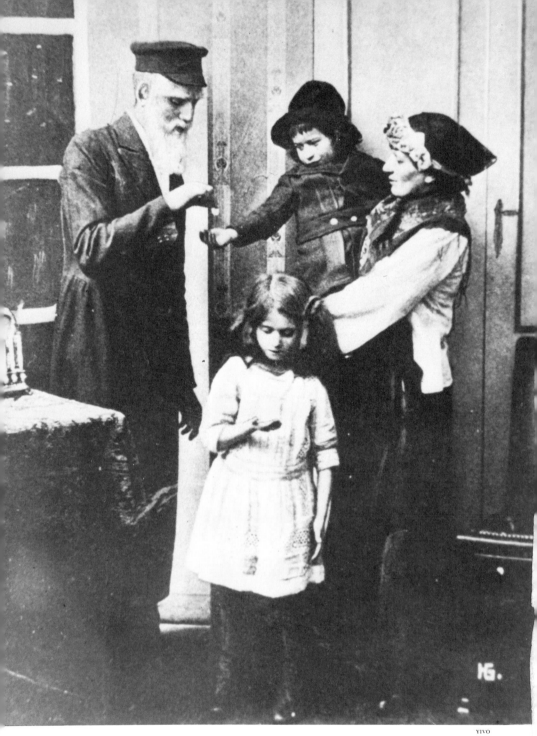

Children receiving Hanukkah money

6
GİFCS

EXCHANGING gifts is one way Hanukkah helps to brighten the winter. Originally only teachers, students, and children received gifts, and the gift was always Hanukkah gelt, or money. It was given to spread light and joy, encourage studying, and hasten the coming of the *Messiah*.

In Eastern Europe, children were allowed to visit their many relatives to ask for gelt. Since this was often the only money they would get all year, their excitement at Hanukkah was tremendous. As with every Jewish holiday, the poor were also given food and money at Hanukkah.

In the United States, people usually give gifts instead of gelt on Hanukkah, probably because of the Christian custom of giving presents at Christmas. One way to preserve the special character of the holiday is to give Hanukkah gifts that are

Israel Hanukkah coins, 1970

rooted in the Jewish tradition. Hanukkah celebrates a rededication of the Temple, and certain gifts can help to rededicate
Jewish life.

A simple but much appreciated gift is personally minted
Hanukkah gelt that offers your services to whomever you give
your gift. For example, the gelt can be your promise to wash
the dishes, baby-sit, or walk the dog. Cut circles from gold
and silver wrapping paper, using a tea cup as a guide for the
gold paper and a juice glass for the silver paper. For a big favor
use the bigger gold circle, and for a smaller favor use the
smaller silver circle. With a marker, write on the face of the
coin: "THIS COIN IS GOOD FOR . . ." (whatever you offer).

A decorative dreidel bank for real Hanukkah gelt is a useful
gift and, because it looks like a dreidel, it will be remembered
as a Hanukkah gift. Take a half-gallon milk carton and cut off
the bottom 3¾ inches (9.52 centimeters) of the length. This will

make a cube. Then cut from the discarded part a square to fit on top of the cube, and tape it in place. Turn the carton over, so the bottom becomes the top. Cut a slit 2 inches (5 centimeters) long for the money to be put through when the bank is finished. The tape can be cut later if you want to get the money out. From what's still left of the discarded part of the carton, cut a rectangle 2 inches (5 centimeters) wide by 1 inch (2.5 centimeters) long. Roll this lengthwise into a stick and tape it to the top. This will be the spinner on the dreidel. To make the carton look pretty, cover each side with colored squares of construction paper (3¾ by 3¾ inches, or 9.52 by 9.52 centimeters). Use white glue for pasting the squares to the sides. Then, paint the Hebrew letters **נ** (*nun*), **ג** (*gimmel*), **ה**(*he*), and **שׁ** (*shin*), one on each side. Poster paint or marker pens show up clearly.

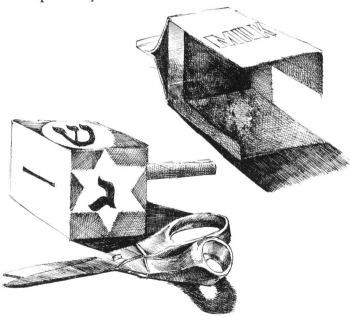

The eraser print blocks described on page 61 can be used to make stationery for your teacher or friends. Take several sheets of white typing paper, fold them in quarters, and cut along the creases. Stamp year-round designs like the star, the lion, the elephant, and the candle around the edges.

A good family gift is a *mezuzah*, which is hung or glued onto the right doorpost at the entrance to a Jewish home. It means the family is dedicated to Jewish ideals just as the Maccabees were when they rededicated the Temple in 165 B.C.E. Its presence also serves as a reminder to obey God's laws away from home as well as in the house.

The mezuzah itself is a container for a small piece of parchment with the handwritten words of the verse from the Torah that begins "Hear, O Israel, the Lord our God, the Lord is One," the deepest of all Jewish prayers. As they enter and leave the house, some people touch the mezuzah with their fingertips and then kiss their fingers.

Half a walnut shell or a sea shell makes a lovely natural mezuzah case. The letter *shin* should show on the mezuzah, because it is the first letter of *Shaddai*, meaning "God Almighty." You can write this with a felt-tip marker on the shell. Put the parchment, which can be bought at a synagogue, in the shell, and paste a piece of cardboard to the back of it with white glue. This backing should be the same size as the shell but should extend a half-inch (1.27 centimeters) beyond the top and bottom. Drive a nail through the top and bottom of the cardboard, so that the mezuzah is attached securely to the doorpost.

The rabbis said that a mezuzah is a great treasure, because most treasures you have to guard, but a mezuzah guards you.

Giant menorah, New York City, 1978

7
CELEBRATIONS

. . . Let us exalt His name together.

PSALMS 34:4

HANUKKAH began as a small holiday, but is now the best-known Jewish holiday. The reason for its popularity is partly because of its cheeriness, but mostly because it falls close to the Christmas season. In the United States at Christmas, schools are closed, shop windows are filled with wonderful toys, and television offers dozens of Christmas specials. In short, Christmas creates a national holiday spirit.

For American Jews, the Christmas season causes problems. All year long they feel the same as everyone around them, but at Christmas they feel different and left out. They want to celebrate just like everyone else.

The Hellenized Jews faced a similar dilemma, because of the appeal of the Greek culture around them. How much can a minority people borrow from a major culture without los-

71

ing its identity? Occasionally, American Jews have tried to answer this question with funny solutions. They end up with a "Hanukkah bush" and blue-and-white stockings on the mantel.

The confusion is understandable, but the question is more than whether to celebrate Christmas if you're Jewish. It's a question of not being able to do everything. In America there are many choices, and people think they can do everything— but this is not true. If a five-year-old child asked to have two birthday parties, his own *and* his friend's birthday, you'd laugh and tell him that he can't have his friend's party, he can only have his own. In the same way, Jews can appreciate a Christian's joy and happiness at Christmas, even visit a friend's Christmas party, but also know that the holiday is not theirs.

Even before the big American Hanukkah, Jews enjoyed celebrating Hanukkah in nearly every country of the world. Two thousand years ago, Hanukkah celebrations took place in Jerusalem. There were grand national festivals, with torch parades in the streets. After the parades were stopped by ruling kings who did not like the fact that Hanukkah celebrated a rebellion, the Hanukkah ceremony moved indoors. The hanukkiyyah took the place of torches.

Until fifty years ago, Middle Eastern Jewish children burned puppets of Antiochus, shouting "Antiochus! Antiochus!", and then put out the fire with water as a plea for needed rain. It was part of a larger celebration in which menorahs were lighted in the morning. Then everyone had a picnic. Because the people were poor, the menorahs were often as simple as eggshell halves with olive oil and wicks. Hanukkah

Children dancing around water tank on Hanukkah in Israel

meant eight days of visiting friends, having parties, and playing games.

Even though the celebrations varied from country to country, two things remained the same: the lighting of candles and
the fact that it was a family celebration. There were prayers
and candlelighting in the synagogue, but mainly the holiday
was observed at home.

For the poorest Jews in Polish ghettos, Hanukkah was a
small escape from their dismal, hard lives. Schools were
closed, and mothers returned early from their stores to light
candles and fry latkes. Everyone took time to enjoy the
beauty of the candles. Although the adults thought of Hanukkah as a children's holiday, the parents who played
checkers, chess, and listened to concerts during Hanukkah
were happy, too. They warmed themselves with this hope:
The Jewish people still had one hidden vessel of oil—they
weren't dry and empty yet. One day the Maccabees would
rise again.

The Jews of Eastern Europe came close to dying out in
World War II, but they still lit Hanukkah candles. It gave them
courage to fight against the enemy. In the concentration
camps, the inmates saved morsels of fat from their meager
food, and pulled threads from their uniforms for wicks. Half a
raw potato was used as a menorah and a dreidel was carved
from a shoe. Not all of these Jews were religious. It was a
matter of loyalty, of not giving in to the Nazis—just as Hannah
and her sons didn't give in to Antiochus.

When the Holocaust ended, six million Jews, nearly the
total European Jewish population, had been killed. Those who
survived were homeless and did not want to return to their
homelands. So many of them left for Israel to set up a Jewish

Torch relay in Modin, Israel

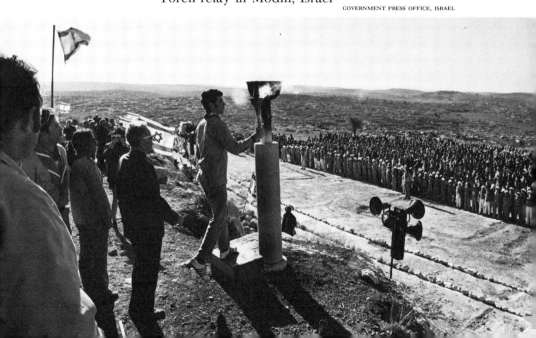

state. It was the first time in 2,000 years that the Jews ruled themselves again. For those Jews, Hanukkah became a very important holiday. The struggles of the Maccabees and their willingness to die for their beliefs had special meaning to these Israelis. They had survived the death camps and had fought in 1948 against the Arabs and the British for their right to be an independent nation.

They were outnumbered and ill-equipped but, like the Maccabees, the weak prevailed over the strong. Some say it was the finger of God that saved them. Others say it was simply that they *had* to win. Their survival was at stake.

Hanukkah is a national holiday in Israel, just as the Fourth of July is a national holiday in the United States. It is a great public festival, and the spirit of the Maccabees is everywhere. Before Hanukkah, students have parties, present plays, and sing Hanukkah songs. During Hanukkah, schools close, menorahs are lit on top of tall buildings, and parties go on everywhere. Dreidel, called *sevivon* in Hebrew, is played as it is here, but with one exception. The letters are *nun, gimmel, he,* and *pe,* to stand for *Nes gadol hayah po*—"A great miracle happened here."

The highlight of the national celebration is a relay race from Modin. Burning torches are carried to Jerusalem's Western Wall, which is all that is left of the Temple. One runner begins in Modin, passes the torch to another along the way, until finally a torchbearer reaches the wall. He gives the torch to the chief rabbi, who uses it to light the first light of the giant hanukkiyyah.

In the Soviet Union, Jews have no such celebration. Their government forbids them any religious observance and does not permit them to make Hanukkah candles. For sixty years,

First light on a menorah at the Western Wall

the U.S.S.R. has tried to erase Judaism from its country, just as Antiochus tried to do 2,100 years ago. When a family is able to smuggle in a few candles from Israel, it treats them like gold. Russian Jews today know very well that they are Jewish, since they are denied jobs and schooling because of it. Yet most don't know a single letter of Hebrew. Many light candles, but don't know why.

Hanukkah is a vital holiday for Jews living in America for two reasons. First, the United States was founded on the principle the Maccabees fought for—religious freedom.

Second, Hanukkah helps American Jews feel close to the proud past of its people. One of the best ways to sense this kinship is by gathering with family and friends on Hanukkah.

A party on one of the eight nights helps create the spirit of Hanukkah. Ask everyone to bring a menorah for the candle-lighting. Put them all on a table, turn off the lights, and light the candles together. While the candles burn, think about how it feels to celebrate together, and about the importance of families and friends. Judah Maccabee learned from his father to be brave, and got support from his brothers to fight Antiochus.

Hanukkah is a good time to find out about your family's history. Think of the burning candles as if they were a campfire around which each person tells a tale about his or her past. You might hear stories that remind you of the Hanukkah story. If you're lucky enough to have grandparents who were born in Europe, let them begin. The struggles of the poor, uneducated Jewish immigrants made them heroic in a different way from the Maccabees. It took great spirit and courage to come to America, and these immigrants saw as a miracle the success enjoyed by their children and grandchildren.

If your friends are with you, let them tell of their background, and you can compare your family tree with theirs. The fact that Jews are here to tell their story 2,100 years after the Maccabees' victory is a miracle, too.

8
hANUKKAh FUN

What's the best holiday? Hanukkah, of course.
You don't go to heder for eight days in a row,
you eat pancakes everyday, spin your dreidel
to your heart's content and from all sides
money comes pouring in. What holiday can be
better than that?

SHOLEM ALEICHEM

BECAUSE they believed in mental gymnastics, the rabbis encouraged puzzles on Hanukkah. As mentioned earlier, they
were called *kattoves,* number puzzles that always had the
same answer: 44.

In place of kattoves, here are a variety of puzzles and
riddles to test how alert you are on Hanukkah after games and
latkes. The answers start on page 82.

STINKY PINKY

A stinky pinky is a word riddle. The answer must consist of an adjective and a noun that rhyme. For example: What is Hanukkah gelt? Dandy candy! If the two words of the answer have only one syllable each, the answer is called a "stink pink."

What is a stink pink for a controlled fire?

A stinky pinky for a wrecker of light?

A stinky pinky for Lysias?

A stink pink for a Hanukkah candle?

A stink pink for a welterweight boxing match?

HANUKKAH RIDDLES

What has Popeye to do with Hanukkah?

Why can't you light Hanukkah candles in the dark?

How are some menorahs like cars?

What is in the middle of a dreidel?

SCRAMBLED WORDS

These words have something to do with the meaning of Hanukkah. Can you unscramble them?

HATCOUSIN
HAMRONE
REDLIDE

CODE

Can you deciper these famous quotes from the Hanukkah story?

DSLVEVI RH ULI GSV OLIW, ULOOLD NV!
Z TIVZG NRIZXOV SZKKVMVW GSVIV.

WORD COUNT

How many words can you make from the letters of these words? (No proper nouns and no plurals.)

Mattathias
Miracle
Rededication

ANSWERS

STINKY PINKY

tame flame
candle vandal
zero hero
bright light
light fight

HANUKKAH RIDDLES

His girlfriend's name is Olive Oyl.
Because you light them in the hanukkiyyah.
They both burn oil.
The letter *i*.

SCRAMBLED WORDS

ANTIOCHUS
MENORAH
DREIDEL

CODE

Key to code: A=Z, B=Y, C=X, etc.

Whoever is for the Lord, follow me!
A great miracle happened there.

WORD COUNT

Mattathias

am	ash	mash	saith	asthma
as	hat	mast	smith	tatami
at	him	math		
is	hit	mist		
it	mat	mitt		
	sat	sham		
	sit	that		
		this		

Miracle

am	ace	acme	mile	camel	malice	reclaim
me	ail	calm	mire	claim	carmel	
	air	came	rail	clear		
	ale	care	real	cream		
	arc	clam	ream	realm		
	are	cram				
	aim	lace				
	cam	lair				
	car	lame				
	ear	liar				
	elm	lice				
	era	lime				
	ice	mace				
	ire	mail				
	lam	male				
	mar	mare				
	ram	mica				
	rim	mice				

Rededication

ad	act	acid	cared	action	candied
at	add	arid	cider	addict	diction
do	ade	card	crate	canter	trained
in	arc	care	creed	cantor	
it	ate	cart	cried	carton	addition
on	can	cent	crone	cinder	dedicate
or	cat	cite	dance	dancer	indicate
to	cod	coin	dread	dander	
	con	core	dried	decent	addiction
	cot	corn	drone	editor	direction
	den	dare	edict	entice	
	did	dart	enter	entire	
	din	date	irate	indeed	
	don	dead	orate	notice	
	dot	dear	radio	ordain	
	ear	deed	trace	ornate	
	eat	dent	trade	ration	
	end	dice	train	recant	
	eon	dint	tread	recent	
	era	dire	trend	recite	
	ice	dirt	tried	redone	
	ion	done		tender	
	net	dote		trained	
	nit	earn		trance	
	nod	edit			
	nor	iced			
	not	into			
	one	Iran			
	ran	need			
	rat	nice			
	red	node			

rid	note
rod	race
tan	raid
ten	rain
tin	rant
ton	rate
	read
	redo
	rend
	rent
	rice
	rind
	riot
	tear
	tend
	tide
	tied
	tine
	tone
	tree

AFTERWORD

I WANT this book to be useful as well as informative. My hope is that you will find something in here to do each night of Hanukkah—playing, eating, thinking, singing—as the candles burn. Being Jewish has to do with deed, not creed. In other words, it's the doing, not only the knowing, that matters. There are many reasons for lighting the candles, but the most important thing is to light them. Then you will have moved the holiday from your mind to your heart and hand.

GLOSSARY

B.C.E.—Before the Common Era. Christians use the term B.C. (Before Christ).

BRIT—The ritual of circumcision. The word means covenant or contract.

CIRCUMCISION—Ritual performed on Jewish males eight days after birth.

DIONYSUS—Greek god of wine.

DREIDEL (Yiddish)—A spinning top used in Hanukkah games.

GELT (Yiddish)—Money traditionally given during Hanukkah.

GIMMEL—Hebrew letter found on the dreidel.

HANUKKAH—Dedication; the Feast of Dedication or the Festival of Lights.

HANUKKIYYAH—A candelabrum with nine branches used for Hanukkah. (Plural: hanukkiyyot)

HASIDIM—The Pietists, or very religious Jews, who refused to become Hellenized in the time of the Maccabees. (Singular: Hasid)

HASMONEAN—Maccabee family.

HAVDALAH—The ceremony at the end of the Sabbath.

HE—Hebrew letter found on the dreidel.

HEDER—Hebrew school in nineteenth-century Europe.

HELLENIZE—To make Greek in style, idea, and belief.

KASHRUT—The system of Jewish laws concerning the preparation and eating of food.

KATTOVES—Number riddles played on Hanukkah.

KISLEV—Ninth month of the Hebrew calendar.

LATKES (Yiddish)—Potato pancakes.

MACCABEE—Refers to Judah and his family; also means "hammer."

MENORAH—A candelabrum used for religious purposes. A Hanukkah menorah has nine branches; a synagogue menorah has seven branches.

MESSIAH—The redeemer and savior.

MEZUZAH—A container holding holy writing, to be placed on right doorpost of a Jewish home. (Plural: mezuzot)

MIDRASH—A legend or tale told by the rabbis.

MITZVAH—Something God commands a person to do. (Plural: mitzvot)

NUN—Hebrew letter found on the dreidel.

PIETISTS—See Hasidim.

PTOLEMISTS—Egyptian rulers.

SELEUCIDS—Syrian rulers.

SEVIVON—The Hebrew term for dreidel.

SHABBAT—The Sabbath, or day of rest.

SHADDAI—The Almighty; God.

SHAMMASH—The "servant" candle of the hanukkiyyah, used to light the eight Hanukkah candles.

SHIN—Hebrew letter found on the dreidel.

SUFGANIYYOT—Israeli doughnuts. (Singular: sufganiyyah)

SUKKOT—Fall harvest festival.

TEMPLE—Holy place for prayer and public celebration of holidays and festivals.

TISHRI—Seventh month of the Hebrew calendar.

TORAH—The first five books of the Bible; guidance, direction.

ZECHARIAH—A book of the Bible, named after a Hebrew prophet.

ZEUS—Chief of the Greek gods.

SUGGESTED READING

Joyce Becker, *Jewish Holiday Crafts* (Hebrew Publishing Co., N.Y., 1977; paperback)

Elias Bickerman, *From Ezra to the Last of the Maccabees* (Schocken Books, Inc., N.Y., 1949)

Theodore Gaster, *Festivals of the Year* (William Morrow & Co., Inc., N.Y., 1972)

Philip Goodman, *The Hanukkah Anthology* (Jewish Publication Society of America, Philadelphia, 1976)

Howard Greenfeld, *Chanukah* (Holt, Rinehart & Winston, N.Y., 1976)

Mae Shafter Rockland, *The Hanukkah Book* (Schocken Books, Inc., N.Y., 1977)

David Rosenberg, *A Blazing Fountain* (Schocken Books, Inc., N.Y., 1978)

Hayyim Schauss, *The Jewish Festivals* (Schocken Books, Inc., N.Y., 1978)

Richard Siegel, *The First Jewish Catalog* (Jewish Publication Society of America, 1973)

iNDEX

93